Hey YOU'RE SO Great

Hey You're So Great: Inspirational and Motivational Coloring Book.Positive Quotes and Stress Relief for Adults.
ISBN: 9798422986286
For more informations and to stay updated on new coloring books visit our website at www.coloringbookkim.com

Hey
YOU'RE SO
Great

DO MORE
OF
what makes
YOU
Happy

You can
Do more
THAN you
Think

YOU
are all
KINDS
OF
Amazing

Never
STOP
Dreaming

DON'T
stress
DO YOUR BEST
FORGET
THE
Rest

THE ONLY WAY
TO DO
GREAT WORK
IS TO LOVE WHAT
YOU DO

BE
happy
AND
smile

IT'S
Never
TOO Late TO
Start SOME-
THING
New

Never forget what you are

Let YOUR
LIGHT
shine

Be Real not Perfect

Remember
YESTERDAY
Dream
TOMORROW
Live
TODAY

Be
PROUD
OF
Yourself
FOR HOW
HARD
you're trying

BE SILLY
BE HONEST
BE KIND

Be
SOMEBODY
WHO Makes
EVERYBODY
FEEL LIKE
A
Somebody

Be Kind
It's
COOLER
than being
COOL

Collect
moments
not
things

Be a
Rainbow
in someone
else's cloud

GO WHERE YOU *feel* THE MOST ALIVE

WEIRD
IS A
Side-effect
OF BEING
AWESOME

You Are
Somebody's
reason
To Smile

Find
joy
IN THE
Simple
things

YOU'RE
Bigger
THAN
YOUR
PROBLEM

TODAY
is the
PERFECT
DAY
to be
HAPPY

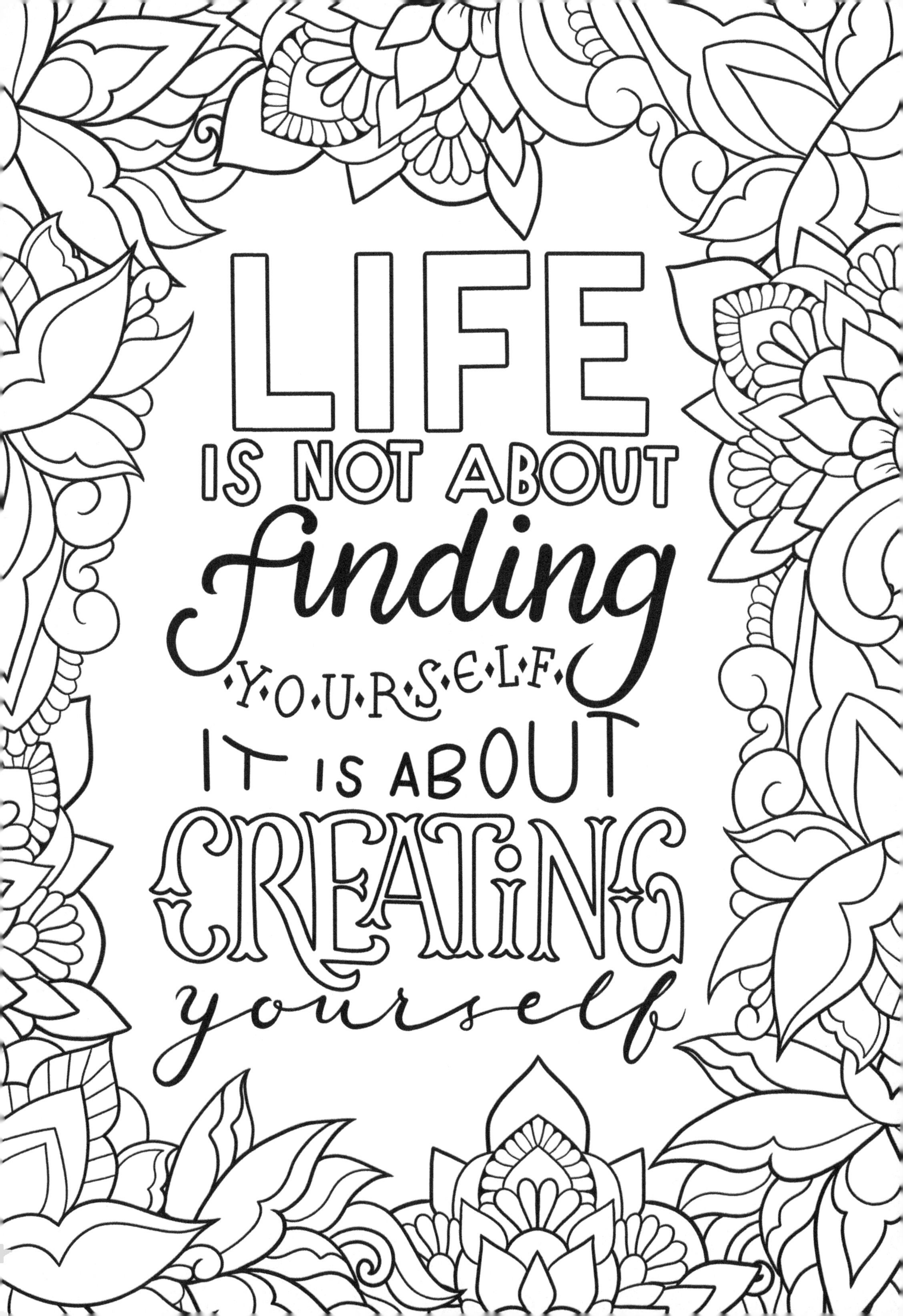
LIFE
IS NOT ABOUT
finding
YOURSELF
IT IS ABOUT
CREATING
yourself

YOU'LL
never
WALK
ALONE

FOCUS
ON
WHAT
MATTERS

Life is a gift

WAKE UP EVERY
DAY AND...

Realize that

MEMORIES
takes us back
dreams
TAKES US
FORWARD

work
HARD
DREAM
BIG

I AM W.E.I.R.D.

Wonderful
Exeiting
Interesting
Real
Differnt

Mistakes
ARE THE
Greatest
Teachers

Never
NEVER
never
Give Up!

NEVER
HOPE
FOR IT
WORK
FOR IT

EVERY STORM THAT COMES also COMES TO AN END

Believe
in
yourself

ADD a little
confetti
to each DAY

EVERY
DAY
IS A
Fresh
START

GREAT
things
take
TIME...

YOU'RE
closer
THAN YOU WERE
yesterday

BE
happy
BE
true
BE
lovely
BE
you

Follow
YOUR
DREAMS
THEY KNOW THE
WAY

it's
Okay to
NOT DO IT
All

Good
THINGS
are
GOING
TO
Happen

live
every
Moment

PROBLEMS
ARE NOT
Stop Signs
THEY ARE
GUIDELINES

trust
THE
MAGIC
of new
BEGINNINGS

Believe
that
you can

Learn To Rest Not To Quit

Made in the USA
Middletown, DE
05 April 2022

63649323R00057